Connecticut

by Ed Pell

Consultant:
Jon E. Purmont
Professor of History
Southern Connecticut
State University

Capstone
press
Mankato, Minnesota

Capstone Press
151 Good Counsel Drive • P.O. Box 669 • Mankato, Minnesota 56002
http://www.capstone-press.com

Library of Congress Cataloging-in-Publication Data
Pell, Ed.
    Connecticut/ by Ed Pell
    v. cm. —(Land of liberty)
    Includes bibliographical references and index.
    Contents: About Connecticut—Land, climate and wildlife—History of Connecticut—
Government and politics—Economy and resources—People and culture.
    ISBN 0-7368-1575-9 (hardcover)
    1. Connecticut—Juvenile literature. [1. Connecticut.] I. Title. II.Series.
F94.3 .P45 2003
974.6—dc21   2002011686

Summary: An introduction to the geography, history, government, politics, economy,
resources, people, and culture of Connecticut, including maps, charts, and a recipe.

Editorial Credits
Amanda L. Doering, editor; Jennifer Schonborn, series designer; Linda Clavel, book
    designer; Angi Gahler, illustrator; Karrey Tweten, photo researcher; Eric Kudalis,
    product planning editor

Photo Credits
Cover images: Yale campus, Yale University/Michael Marsland; Connecticut fall scene, Unicorn
    Stock Photos/H.Schmeiser

Blaine Harrington III, 38; Bruce Coleman, Inc./Gene Ahrens, 12–13; Capstone Press/Gary
Sundermeyer, 54; Connecticut Historical Society, 28–29; Corbis/Bettmann, 27, 30, 37, 40;
Corbis/David H. Wells, 51; Fred Atwood, 56; Houserstock, Inc./Christie Parker, 8;
Houserstock, Inc./David G. Houser, 50; Hulton Archive by Getty Images, 23;
Image Finders/Mark Gibson, 36; John Muldoon, 46; Library of Congress, 25; Mae Scanlan, 4;
Marilyn "Angel" Wynn, 18–19, 52; North Wind Picture Archives, 16, 21, 24, 53, 58;
One Mile Up, Inc., 55 (both); PhotoDisc, Inc. 1, 14; Photophile/James Blank, 32;
Paul Rezendez, 42–43, 45, 63; Paul Sutherland Photography/sutherlandstock.com, 15, 57;
U.S. Postal Service, 59; Yale University/Michael Marsland, 48

Artistic Effects
Digital Stock, PhotoDisc, Inc.

1 2 3 4 5 6 08 07 06 05 04 03

Table of Contents

Mystic Seaport offers visitors the chance to see many different kinds of ships such as the one shown above.

Chapter 1

About Connecticut

Mystic Seaport has always been an important place in Connecticut. Fast-sailing clipper ships were built there and sailed from this port. In the 1800s, wooden whaling ships sailed from Mystic Seaport to hunt whales in the Atlantic Ocean.

During the Revolutionary War (1775–1783), sailors watched for British warships from Mystic Seaport. The first submarine, *The American Turtle*, was invented and tested in this area in 1776.

Today, Mystic Seaport is a popular tourist spot. This historical place has the largest nautical museum in North America. The seaport also offers an aquarium, planetarium, shops, and other places to visit. Tourists come to see a model of the slave ship

Amistad. Actual whaling ships, like the *Charles M. Morgan*, can also be seen.

The Constitution State

Connecticut's nickname is the Constitution State. Thomas Hooker's Fundamental Orders and Roger Sherman's famous Connecticut Compromise became models for the current U.S. Constitution and government.

Another nickname given to Connecticut is the Nutmeg State. Connecticut merchants, known as Connecticut Yankees, sold nutmegs. A nutmeg is a small, hard fruit that is ground into spice. The spice is used in pie and other food dishes. The people of Connecticut are sometimes called Nutmeggers or Yankees because of these merchants.

Connecticut is the third smallest state in the country, but it is the 29th largest state in population. Almost 3.5 million people live in the state. Connecticut is the southernmost state in the region called New England. Massachusetts borders Connecticut to the north. Rhode Island is to the east, and New York lies to the west. A part of the Atlantic Ocean called the Long Island Sound lies to Connecticut's south.

Connecticut Cities

MASSACHUSETTS

NEW YORK

RHODE ISLAND

⭐ Hartford

• New Britain

MASHANTUCKET
PEQUOT
RESERVATION

• Waterbury   • Meriden

Mystic
Seaport

New London

• Danbury

• New Haven

Bridgeport •

• Norwalk

Stamford •

Long Island Sound

Long Island
(NEW YORK)

ATLANTIC
OCEAN

Legend

▪ American Indian Reservation

⭐ Capital

• City

○ Feature

Scale
Miles
0   5   10   15   20   25

0 5 10 15 20 25
Kilometers

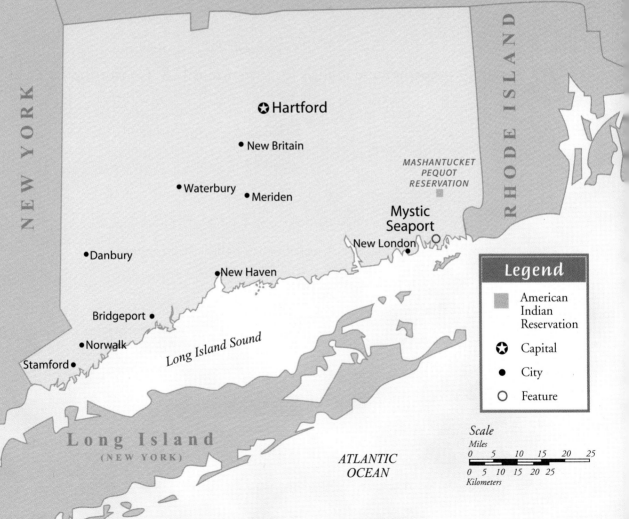

The Appalachian National Scenic Trail runs through the Berkshire Hills. Much of Connecticut's plant life and wildlife can be seen in these hills.

Chapter 2

Land, Climate, and Wildlife

Connecticut's land has four regions. The Eastern and Western Uplands sit on both sides with the flatter Central Lowland between them. The narrow Coastal Lowland runs along the southern border of Connecticut.

Land

The Western Upland is sometimes called the Berkshire Hills. The highest point in the state is located here. Mount Frissell stands 2,380 feet (725 meters) above sea level in the Berkshire Hills.

"*Of all the beautiful towns it has been my fortune to see, Hartford is the chief... You do not know what beauty is if you have not been here.*"
—*Mark Twain*

Forests and farms cover the fields and valleys of the Eastern Upland. Some of the land that was once cleared for farming has been allowed to return to forests. The best farmland is in the Central Lowland. Hartford, the state capital, is located in this area.

The Coastal Lowland is the most populated part of the state. Many people who work in New York City live in this area. The southernmost part of the Coastal Lowland has sandy beaches.

Water

Thousands of years ago, sheets of slow-moving ice called glaciers moved through Connecticut. These glaciers carved out hills and valleys. When the glaciers melted, they filled many lake beds and riverbeds. These rivers include the Housatonic, Naugatuck, Thames, and Connecticut Rivers.

The largest lake in the state, Lake Candlewood, was made by people. Between 1927 and 1929, the Connecticut Light

Connecticut's Land Features

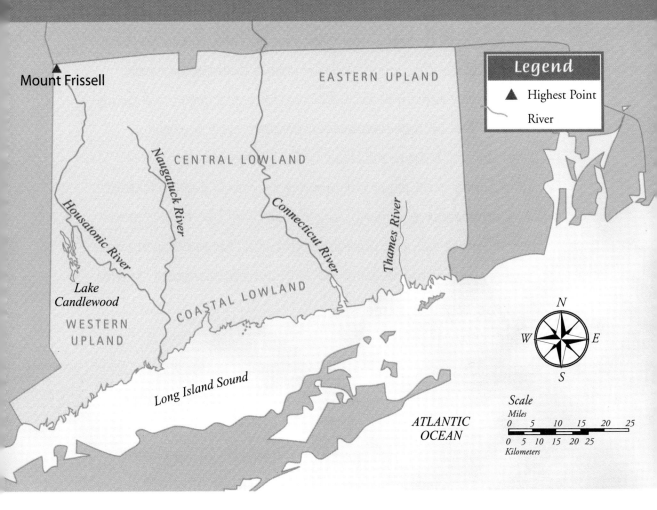

Mount Frissell

EASTERN UPLAND

Legend

▲ Highest Point

~ River

CENTRAL LOWLAND

Naugatuck River

Housatonic River

Connecticut River

Thames River

Lake Candlewood

COASTAL LOWLAND

WESTERN UPLAND

Long Island Sound

ATLANTIC OCEAN

N W E S

Scale

Miles
0 5 10 15 20 25

0 5 10 15 20 25
Kilometers

and Power Company built a dam to provide electricity to the area. The dam held back the waters of the Housatonic River and flooded the Rocky River Valley. This flooding made Lake Candlewood.

Climate

Connecticut's climate varies from one part of the state to the other. Usually the upland hills are cooler than the lowlands. Winters and summers are mild, but the temperature can change quickly. The average summer temperature is 69 degrees Fahrenheit (21 degrees Celsius). The average winter temperature is 28 degrees Fahrenheit (minus 2 degrees Celsius).

Connecticut gets many storms each year. The state is in a belt scientists call the "prevailing westerly." Air moves from west to east where it meets damp air coming from the ocean. Storms are the result.

In winter, storms called northeasters, or nor'easters, hit Connecticut. These storms come in from the North Atlantic Ocean. They bring high winds and a great deal of snow or rain.

Wildlife

Connecticut's hills are home to many kinds of woodland animals like deer and red and gray foxes. Small animals like squirrels, rabbits, raccoons, opossums, groundhogs, and mice also live in the state.

In some areas of the state, coyotes cause trouble. They will attack farm animals and pets. Some coyotes are not afraid

Rich farmland borders much of the Connecticut River.

of people. Coyotes were not originally found in Connecticut. They made their way east and reached the state in the 1950s.

Middlesex County in Connecticut is the only known home of the endangered least shrew. The least shrew is the smallest mammal in North America. These tiny animals are just 3.5 inches (9 centimeters) long. They eat bugs, worms, and snails. This shy animal is rarely seen in the wild. Pollution and farm chemicals threaten the shrew.

Connecticut is also home to many kinds of birds. Nutmeggers may see ospreys along Connecticut's rivers, lakes,

About 3,000 to 5,000 coyotes live in Connecticut.

The Sperm Whale

Connecticut's state animal, the sperm whale, played an important part in the state's history. In the late 1700s, people used whale oil for lamps and candles. Other whale parts, like teeth and stomach bile, were sold to make perfume and other products. The need for these products made whale hunting a large industry in the waters surrounding Connecticut. Overhunting endangered the whales. Today, hunting sperm whales is illegal.

The sperm whale is the largest of the toothed whales. The male can grow to 60 feet (18 meters) in length and weigh up to 45 tons (41 metric tons).

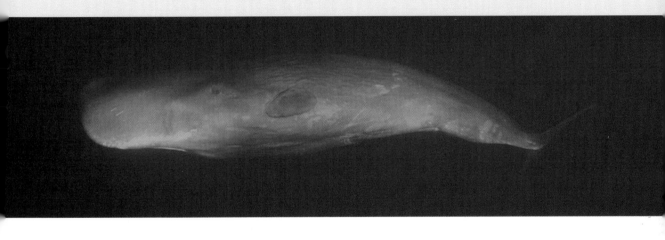

and seashores. The osprey is a large hawk that eats fish. Litter and farm chemicals hurt ospreys. Ospreys are watched and protected by wildlife scientists and volunteers. The number of ospreys in Connecticut is now growing.

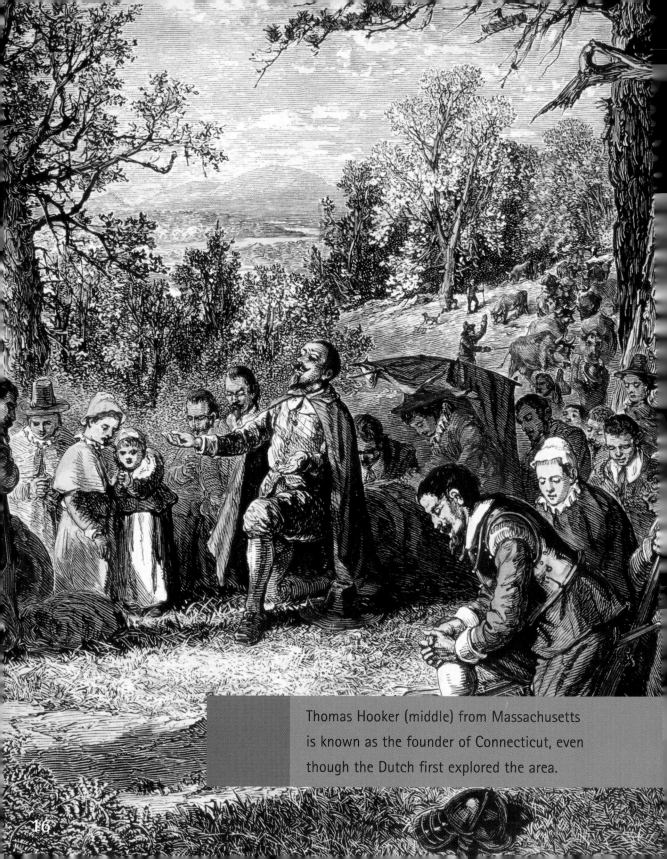

Thomas Hooker (middle) from Massachusetts is known as the founder of Connecticut, even though the Dutch first explored the area.

Chapter 3

History of Connecticut

In 1614, a Dutch explorer named Adriaen Block first arrived in Connecticut. He met the Pequot and the Mohegan tribes of the Algonquin Indians. Block traded furs with the Indians. He drew maps of the area and sailed up what is now called the Connecticut River.

Block claimed the area for the Dutch. In 1633, the Dutch built a small fort called House of Hope. The Dutch never really settled there. They soon deserted the fort.

Massachusetts Settlers

Settlers from Massachusetts came south to Connecticut about the same time the Dutch left. In 1636, Thomas Hooker founded Hartford at the House of Hope. He also founded the villages of Windsor and Wethersfield. These villages became known as the Connecticut Colony. Even though the Dutch built the House of Hope, Hooker is known as the founding father of Connecticut because he built the first permanent settlement there.

The new settlers and the Pequot people did not get along. The Pequot War (1637) soon broke out. The new settlers joined with the Mohegan and Narragansett Indians to attack the Pequots at the village of Mystic. They killed more than 600 Pequot men, women, and children. The Pequots were driven out of the area.

In 1639, the new settlers made a set of laws called the Fundamental Orders. The Fundamental Orders came from one of Thomas Hooker's beliefs. He thought that government should be based only on the agreement of the people being governed by it. The Fundamental Orders became one of the models for the U.S. Constitution.

New Haven Colony

In 1638, a group of planters founded the New Haven colony in southern Connecticut. They bought the land from the Quinnipiac Indians.

Once a small port with Pequot villages, Mystic today is filled with hotels, boats, homes, and tourist attractions. The attack on the Pequot Indians happened at Mystic.

In 1662, England's King Charles II gave Connecticut a royal document called a charter. This charter made the colonists in Connecticut more independent from England. King Charles II put the New Haven colony within Connecticut's borders. The people of New Haven did not want to be a part of Connecticut. They argued for three years before agreeing to join the Connecticut colony. For the next 200 years, the capital switched back and forth every year between New Haven and Hartford.

The Charter Oak

Not everyone in England liked the idea that Connecticut was independent. In 1687, King James II named Sir Edmund Andros the governor of a large part of New England. King James II sent Andros to take away all the charters in New England. Andros arrived in Hartford to take the charter document King Charles II had signed. Without the charter, the colonists could not prove their independence.

Andros and the colonists had a candlelight meeting one night. Suddenly, the room went dark. By the time the candles were relit, the charter was gone. The colonists hid the charter in a hollow oak tree so Andros could not take it away.

This tree is the famous Charter Oak. The Charter Oak fell during a storm in 1856. A monument now marks the spot where the oak stood.

The Revolutionary War

In 1765, the British passed the Stamp Act. The act made colonists pay taxes on books, newspapers, and other

Colonists hid the Connecticut charter in an oak tree so it could not be taken away. The tree became known as the Charter Oak.

"I regret I have but one life to give for my country."

—Nathan Hale of Coventry, Connecticut, Revolutionary War spy

printed materials. Jonathan Trumbull and other citizens of Connecticut joined a group called the Sons of Liberty. The Sons of Liberty fought against British taxes and control. The group felt the taxes were unfair because the colonies had no say in the British government.

The relationship between the colonies and Great Britain grew worse. Many colonists wanted independence from Great Britain. In April 1775, fighting between British troops and colonists broke out in Massachusetts. More than 3,000 men from Connecticut joined the battle. The Revolutionary War had begun. Connecticut offered soldiers, food, guns, clothing, and other goods to the American cause.

The United States of America was created on July 4, 1776. Representatives from the 13 colonies gathered in Philadelphia, Pennsylvania, to sign the Declaration of Independence. Roger Sherman, Samuel Huntington, William Williams, and Oliver Wolcott, all of Connecticut, were among those who signed the Declaration of Independence.

General Putnam

General Israel Putnam of Connecticut was one of the most famous military men of the Revolutionary War. Putnam is remembered for a dangerous escape on horseback near Greenwich. In February 1779, Putnam was chased by British troops. He rode his horse down 70 icy stone steps to escape. The British refused to follow his dangerous attempt. A monument now stands at the spot where he escaped. The place is called Putnam Memorial Park.

In 1787, representatives from each state met to hold the Constitutional Convention in Philadelphia, Pennsylvania. They tried to write a constitution for the new country. They were unable to agree on what sort of legislature they wanted.

The larger states wanted the number of representatives for each state to depend on the population of the state. The smaller states feared they would have no say in governmental matters. They wanted a legislature where each state had an equal number of votes. Neither side was willing to give in to the other's demands.

A Connecticut citizen, Roger Sherman, suggested that the legislature be broken into two equal houses. His suggestion became known as the Connecticut Compromise. The Senate allows each state two senators to represent its interests. The state population determines the number of members in the House of Representatives. Both houses are equal in power.

On January 9, 1788, representatives from Connecticut signed the U.S. Constitution. Connecticut became the fifth state to join the United States.

Roger Sherman's Connecticut Compromise paved the way for the current U.S. legislature.

Eli Whitney set up weapons factories in Connecticut. These factories made guns and ammunition.

Invention and Mass Production

Connecticut is famous for its inventors. In 1793, Eli Whitney invented the cotton gin to separate cotton from its seeds. Whitney manufactured cotton gins, guns, and other goods at his factories in Connecticut. He and other Connecticut inventors also created a way to build many copies of the same product at one time. Called mass production, this method has

Did you know...?
Connecticut was small and did not have much farmland. The state traded manufactured goods. Connecticut's salespeople became known as Yankee peddlers.

shaped modern industry. Before mass production, items were made one at a time.

Whitney and the others made their products out of interchangeable parts. This meant products were put together with identical parts. If a part in a clock or gun broke, a new part could be put in. The mass production process created jobs. Goods were built faster and cheaper. Manufacturing became an important business in Connecticut.

The Civil War

Because Connecticut was a manufacturing state, it had no need for slave labor. The South needed slaves to work on large farms. Most of Connecticut was against slavery. The state sided with the Union when the Southern states withdrew, or seceded, from the country. The Southern states formed the Confederacy. The Confederacy did not want Northern states telling them what to do. They thought each state should make its own laws. In 1861, the Confederacy opened fire on Fort Sumter in South Carolina. This action started the Civil War (1861–1865).

During the Civil War, Connecticut's factories made guns, bullets, and other goods for the military. More than 50,000 men from Connecticut joined the Union Army.

World Wars, Depression, and Disaster

Manufacturing continued to be a major industry in Connecticut following the Civil War. In the late 1800s and early 1900s, many immigrants from Europe came to Connecticut. These immigrants worked in factories and other businesses. Connecticut workers

Many Nutmeggers volunteered their time and energy for the World War I effort. These Red Cross workers are rolling bandages in New Britain.

provided weapons, uniforms, and other war supplies for soldiers in World War I (1914–1918).

The Great Depression (1929–1939) struck the country after the stock market crash of 1929. Many people lost their jobs and their land. It was a difficult time for people in Connecticut and in the United States.

Besides suffering from the economic depression, Connecticut faced severe flooding in the spring of 1936. More than 14 inches (36 centimeters) of rain fell in nine days.

The dam at New Hartford burst. About 14,000 people lost their homes in the flood. Damages cost more than $100 million.

Before the people of Connecticut could recover, the Great Hurricane of 1938 hit the East Coast. The hurricane brought damaging winds and flooding. Many homes, businesses, and boats were destroyed. Hundreds of people died in the storm.

World War II (1939–1945) pulled the United States and Connecticut out of the Great Depression. Once again, Connecticut became the center of manufacturing war supplies.

Water flooded the streets of downtown Hartford during the flood of 1936.

People fled from the main circus tent at the Ringling Brothers Circus in Hartford as it went up in flames. More than 160 people died in the fire.

Factories needed many workers, and people could easily find jobs. More than 200,000 Nutmeggers also served in the military.

Connecticut's troubles were not over. In 1944, people were enjoying a performance of the Ringling Brothers Circus in Hartford. A fire broke out in the main circus tent. More than 160 people died, and hundreds more were hurt.

"It is not enough to profess faith in the democratic process; we must do something about it."

—Ella Grasso, first female governor of Connecticut

In August 1955, Hurricanes Connie and Diane hit the Connecticut area a week apart. The floods caused by the hurricanes killed 77 people and hurt 4,700 others. The floods caused more than $350 million of damage. Floodwaters completely washed away downtown Winsted, Connecticut.

Connecticut Advancements

Even during times of trouble, Connecticut made some big advances. In 1943, Connecticut set up the Inter-Racial Commission. This group was the nation's first civil rights agency. The agency's job was to make sure all people were treated fairly. In 1947, the state made job discrimination against the law.

In the late 1900s, women made advances in Connecticut. In 1974, Ella Grasso became the first woman elected on her own as governor of a U.S. state. Other women had served as governor, but they had taken over for their husbands or were elected after their husbands' term. In 1990, Eunice S. Groark became the first woman elected lieutenant governor of Connecticut.

State lawmakers meet in the capitol in Hartford. The dome of the capitol is covered in gold.

Chapter 4

Government and Politics

Like the U.S. government, the Connecticut state government has three branches. The executive branch carries out laws. The legislative branch proposes laws. The judicial branch interprets laws and tries court cases.

Branches of Government

Voters elect officers in the executive branch. All officers have four-year terms. These officers manage and direct the work of the state government. The governor takes care of the day-to-day operations of government. The governor's office is in the state capitol in Hartford.

The Connecticut legislature is called the General Assembly and includes a senate and a house of representatives. Legislatures help to solve problems by passing laws for the common good.

Members of both the senate and the house of representatives represent their districts based on population. The General Assembly includes 36 state senators and 151 state representatives. Each member of the General Assembly serves a two-year term. A member may not serve in any other state office. The lieutenant governor leads the state senate and can vote to break a tie. The house is led by a speaker, who is elected from among the members.

The judicial branch of government solves problems and carries out justice. It also must define the constitution and the laws of the state. The judicial branch includes the supreme, appellate, superior, and probate courts. The probate court settles questions about wills and trusts. Superior courts handle civil and criminal cases. People who are unhappy with the results of their trial can have the case retried at an appellate court.

Connecticut's Government

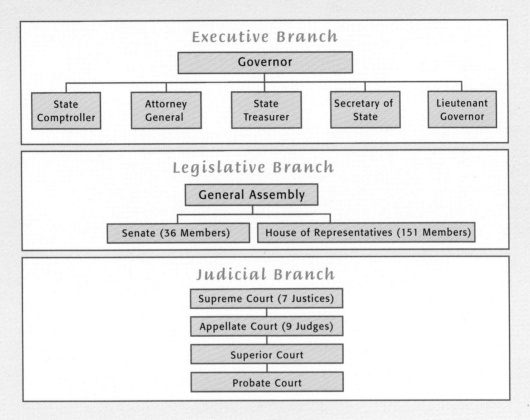

The supreme court is the highest court in the state. This court hears cases that have already been tried by lower courts.

Local and National Government

Eight counties make up Connecticut, but there are no county governments. Below the state level, government consists of 169 towns and cities with local governments.

Like all states, Connecticut voters elect two U.S. Senators. Five U.S. Representatives are also elected. These senators and representatives represent Connecticut's views in Washington, D.C.

Connecticut is known for its stable politics. The state is not strongly either Democratic or Republican. Connecticut citizens support candidates of both parties, plus other independent candidates.

Many state officials work in Hartford's State Legislative Office building.

Ella Grasso

Ella Grasso was the first female governor to be elected in Connecticut. She was also the first female governor in the United States who did not serve after her husband.

Ella Grasso was born in Windsor Locks, Connecticut, in 1919. She graduated from Mount Holyoke College in 1940. Grasso earned a master's degree in 1942. The next year, she became involved in politics by joining the League of Women Voters. She was elected to the state legislature in 1952 and again in 1954.

Grasso was elected as Connecticut Secretary of State three times. She worked for hospital, day care, and civil rights reform.

In 1970 and 1972, Grasso was elected to serve in the U.S. House of Representatives. While in Washington, D.C., she set up a 24-hour toll-free "Ella-Phone" so her voters could reach her. Grasso wanted to bring the government closer to the people. Ordinary people felt at home with her.

In 1974, Grasso was elected governor of Connecticut. She fought for government support for workers, education, and health care. She was reelected in 1978, but poor health forced her to leave office in 1980. She died in 1981. Grasso never lost an election in her 28-year career. Ella Grasso Hall at Western Connecticut State University is named after her.

Manufacturing is Connecticut's main industry. These people are working at a factory that makes airplane engines.

Chapter 5

Economy and Resources

Connecticut is a successful state. Its citizens lead the nation in average personal income. Connecticut's minimum wage is higher than the national standard. The state also has the highest percentage of college graduates.

Manufacturing

Manufacturing has always been important to Connecticut's economy. Connecticut was an early manufacturing center. Factories in the state made clocks, watches, guns, boats, and clothing.

Connecticut is still a leader in manufacturing. Today, rocket motors, space suits, submarines, airplane engines, small boats, and other products are made in Connecticut. The state also makes chemical products, electrical equipment, and machine tools. Factories in Connecticut make machines that are used in other states to manufacture products.

Connecticut's Inventors

Connecticut's most valuable resource has always been its inventors. The portable typewriter was invented in the state in 1843. In 1844, Charles Goodyear discovered how to make rubber stronger. The stronger rubber would not melt on hot

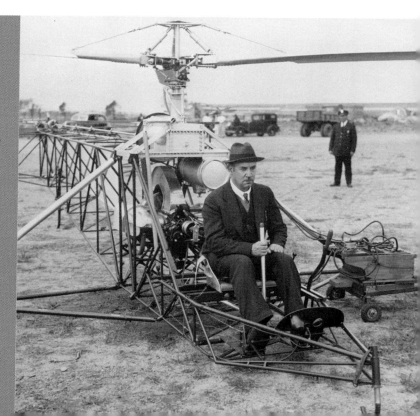

In 1939, Igor Sikorsky built and tested his helicopter in Bridgeport, Connecticut.

days or crack in cold weather. Elias Howe invented the sewing machine in 1846, and in 1853, the first ice-making machine was introduced. In 1858, the first can opener was manufactured.

The 20th century was also filled with inventors. Igor Sikorsky, a Russian immigrant, invented the first working helicopter in 1939. The first nuclear-powered submarine was built and launched in the state in 1954. In 1982, Dr. Robert Jarvik of Stamford invented the first artificial heart.

Insurance

The U.S. insurance industry was born in Hartford. The first accident insurance in the country was sold in 1795 in Connecticut. By 1810, the ancestor of today's ITT Hartford Group was selling policies. Most of these policies were to protect people from risks while traveling.

Insurance companies in Connecticut paid most of the claims after the Great Fire of 1871 in Chicago. This disaster left 100,000 people without homes. Damages from the fire cost more than $200 million.

Insurance continues to be a major industry in Connecticut. Today, more than 100 insurance companies have their headquarters in Connecticut.

Agriculture

Agriculture is a small part of Connecticut's total economic output, but it is still important. Shade tobacco is one of the

largest crops. It is called shade tobacco because the plants are covered with tents to shield them from the sun.

Other agricultural products such as eggs, milk, and beef cattle are produced in Connecticut. Greenhouse plants and flowers are Connecticut's largest agricultural products. The state also produces forest products, such as hardwood lumber.

Tourism

Tourists spend $4 billion a year in Connecticut. Connecticut's scenery is some of New England's most

Although agriculture is not a large part of Connecticut's economy, the state does produce eggs, milk, and other agricultural products. This photo shows a dairy farm in Lyme, Connecticut.

beautiful. People come from all over the world to experience Connecticut's New England charm. Visitors can find many of the colonial landmarks and historic places that make New England famous.

Tourists also come to Connecticut for sports and relaxation. Connecticut has dozens of public golf courses. Boating, fishing, sailing, and swimming are also popular with tourists. Thousands of people visit Connecticut's beaches every year.

Natural Resources

Connecticut has natural resources such as stone and minerals. Sandstone, copper, and graphite are found in the Central Lowlands. Sandstone, also called brownstone, comes in many colors. The stone was used in many older buildings and for grave markers. Graphite is a mineral used in pencil lead.

Many tourists visit Connecticut's beaches. New London Beach is one of the most famous beaches in Connecticut.

The Main Street, U.S.A. Festival is celebrated every year in New Britain.

Chapter 6

People and Culture

Almost all of Connecticut's first immigrants were from England. Irish people came to the area after the Revolutionary War. Italians came in great numbers between 1900 and 1916. Germans and Russians arrived between 1880 and 1919. Many of these immigrants came looking for jobs in Connecticut. Today, the state has a mix of people.

Irish, Scottish, and Italian immigrants have festivals to celebrate their cultures. Food, games, music, and dancing are part of the entertainment at these festivals.

Other festivals and celebrations are held in Connecticut. Nutmeggers celebrate the Main Street, U.S.A. Festival in New Britain. The River Festival is celebrated in Hartford.

Nutmeggers

About 30 percent of all people living in Connecticut in 1910 were born in a different country. That number had fallen to 9 percent by 1970. Today, about 10 percent of the state's residents were born overseas. Most Nutmeggers have European backgrounds. Most of Connecticut's population is white, but large populations of African Americans and Hispanic Americans live in Hartford, New Haven, and Bridgeport.

The Yale campus in New Haven covers more than 800 acres (324 hectacres) of land and includes more than 255 buildings.

Connecticut's Ethnic Backgrounds

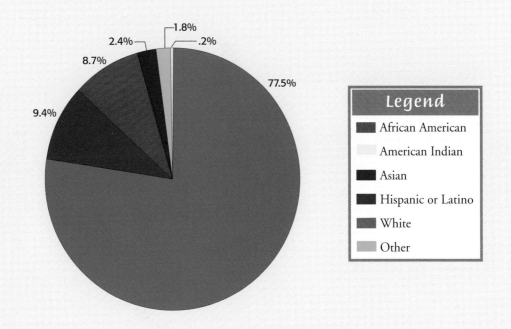

1.8%
.2%
2.4%
8.7%
9.4%
77.5%

Legend
- African American
- American Indian
- Asian
- Hispanic or Latino
- White
- Other

Education

In 1701, the Collegiate School in Killingworth, Connecticut, was founded. In 1716, it moved to New Haven, where today it is known as Yale. Yale is one of the country's oldest and best-known universities.

Quality education has always been important to Connecticut. Nutmeggers spend about $3,000 more per student in public schools than the average state. An average Connecticut classroom has 14 students, while the country's average is almost 17 students.

The Goodspeed Opera House in East Haddam presents many plays and musicals throughout the year.

The Sport of Frisbee

New Haven's college students enjoyed the pies at Frisbie's bakery. They liked the empty pie tins even more. The students began throwing the empty pie tins as a game in 1920. This game became the sport of Frisbee. The plastic pie-tin-shaped disks of today are still called Frisbees.

Theater

Connecticut's citizens enjoy a rich cultural life. Connecticut is famous for the arts and has many theaters. Many plays are performed at The Long Wharf Theatre in New Haven. The shows are performed there before going on to New York. The Goodspeed Opera House in East Haddam puts on several shows a year.

Museums

Connecticut is home to many famous museums. The U.S. Coast Guard Museum celebrates the men and women who have kept America's coasts safe. Visitors to the USS *Nautilus* Museum can explore America's first nuclear submarine.

The Peabody Museum of Natural History at Yale holds famous fossils of dinosaurs. O. C. Marsh, who worked for the Peabody, discovered and named many kinds of animals.

The Wadsworth Atheneum Museum of Art is located in Hartford. This museum is considered one of the finest art museums in the country. Other art museums can be found in Norwich, New London, New Britain, and New Haven.

The Mashantucket Pequot Museum brings the Indian nation to life. The museum offers films, exhibits, and artifacts to show what life was like for these American Indians.

The Mashantucket Pequot Museum has several lifelike exhibits that demonstrate how these American Indians in Connecticut lived.

Mark Twain

Author Mark Twain lived in Connecticut for many years. One of his most famous books is a tribute to his clever neighbors. Twain's book is called *A Connecticut Yankee in King Arthur's Court*. The book has been the basis of many movies and TV shows.

Twain's house in Hartford is a state monument. Many tourists visit every year. Twain died in the town of Redding, Connecticut, in 1910. The city of Hartford holds a celebration in his honor every year.

Connecticut itself is a museum of the country's history. Many important people and ideas came from Connecticut's past. The state continues to lead the country in many ways. Nutmeggers have worked hard to preserve their heritage and advance their state's future.

Recipe: Nutmeg Muffins

Connecticut is known as the Nutmeg State. The people of Connecticut are sometimes called Nutmeggers. This recipe uses nutmeg to make tasty muffins.

Ingredients

2 cups (480 mL) flour
3 tablespoons (45 mL) sugar
1 tablespoon (15 mL) baking powder
1 teaspoon (5 mL) ground nutmeg
¼ teaspoon (1.2 mL) salt
2 large eggs
1 cup (240 mL) milk
4 tablespoons (60 mL) butter or margarine

Equipment

paper baking cups
muffin pan
measuring spoons
measuring cups
large mixing bowl
mixing spoon
medium mixing bowl
whisk
oven mitts

What You Do

1. Preheat the oven to 375°F (190°C).
2. Place one paper baking cup in each hole of the muffin pan and set pan aside.
3. Mix flour, sugar, baking powder, nutmeg, and salt in the large mixing bowl. Mix well.
4. Break eggs into the medium mixing bowl and throw away eggshells.
5. Add milk and butter to the eggs.
6. Whisk eggs, milk, and butter until well blended.
7. Pour egg, milk, and butter mixture over the dry ingredients in the large mixing bowl.
8. Mix all ingredients with a spoon until ingredients are moistened.
9. Spoon batter into baking cups.
10. Bake for 15–20 minutes or until lightly browned and springy to the touch.
11. Let muffins cool 10–20 minutes before eating.

Makes 12 muffins

Connecticut's Flag and Seal

Connecticut's Flag

Adopted in 1897, Connecticut's flag features a white shield on a blue background. The shield is bordered in gold and silver with three grapevines in the center. Below, a banner says "Qui Transtulit Sustinet," Latin for "He, who transplanted, still sustains."

Connecticut's Seal

The original seal, created in 1639, showed a field of grapevines and the state motto that the flag bears. Over time, the number of grapevines has been reduced to just three. The words "Sigillum Reipublicae Connecticutensis," which is Latin for "Seal of the State of Connecticut," were added around 1784.

Almanac

Nicknames: Constitution State, Nutmeg State

Population: 3,405,565 (U.S. Census 2000)
Population rank: 29th

Capital: Hartford

Largest cities: Bridgeport, New Haven, Hartford, Stamford, Waterbury

Agriculture

Agricultural products: Tobacco, greenhouse plants, milk, eggs

Climate

Average winter temperature: 28 degrees Fahrenheit (minus 2 degrees Celsius)

Average summer temperature: 69 degrees Fahrenheit (21 degrees Celsius)

Average annual precipitation: 44 inches (112 centimeters)

Geography

Area: 4,845 square miles (12,549 square kilometers)
Size rank: 48th

Highest point: Mount Frissell, 2,380 feet (725 meters) above sea level

Lowest point: The beach along Long Island Sound, sea level

Mountain laurel

Economy

Natural resources: Sandstone, copper, graphite

Types of industry: Metal products, machinery, chemicals, engines, insurance

Symbols

Animal: Sperm whale

Bird: American robin

Flower: Mountain laurel

Symbols

Hero: Nathan Hale

Heroine: Prudence Crandall

Song: "Yankee Doodle"

Tree: Charter Oak

Government

First governor: Samuel Huntington

Statehood: January 9, 1788; 5th state

U.S. Representatives: 5

U.S. Senators: 2

U.S. electoral votes: 7

Counties: 8

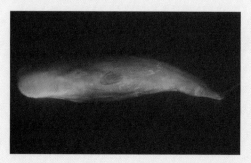

Sperm whale

Timeline

State History

1614
Dutch explorer Adriaen Block sails up the Connecticut River and maps the region.

1637
The Pequot War is fought between settlers and the Pequot Indians.

1639
The Connecticut constitution, the Fundamental Orders, is written.

1787
Roger Sherman's Connecticut Compromise paves the way for ratification of the U.S. Constitution.

1788
Connecticut becomes the fifth state.

1810
The first insurance company is founded in Hartford.

1880–1919
Many immigrants arrive in Connecticut.

U.S. History

1775–1783
American colonists fight for independence from the British in the Revolutionary War.

1861–1865
The North and the South fight the Civil War.

1620
Pilgrims settle in North America.

1914–1918
World War I is fought. The United States enters the war in 1917.

1938
The Great
Hurricane hits
Connecticut.

1954
The first
nuclear
submarine is
invented in
Groton.

1974
The first female
governor of
Connecticut, Ella
Grasso, is elected.

1939
The first
working
helicopter is
invented in
Connecticut.

1955
Hurricanes Connie and
Diane hit Connecticut
one week apart.

1982
The first
artificial
heart is
invented in
Stamford.

1939–1945
World War II is
fought. The United
States enters the war
in 1941.

1964
Congress passes the
Civil Rights Act, making
discrimination illegal.

2001
On September 11,
terrorists attack the
World Trade Center
and the Pentagon.

1929–1939
The Great
Depression hits
the United States.

Words to Know

charter (CHAR-tur)—a document that gives rights to a group of people; Connecticut received a charter from King Charles II.

Confederacy (kuhn-FED-ur-uh-see)—the 11 states that left the Union during the Civil War

glacier (GLAY-shur)—a thick sheet of slow-moving ice

graphite (GRAF-ite)—a mineral used in pencil lead

mass production (MASS pruh-DUHK-shuhn)—a way to make many identical items at one time

nor'easter (NOR-EE-stur)—a storm that comes in from the Atlantic Ocean

nutmeg (NUHT-meg)—a spice that is ground and put into pies and other dishes

secede (si-SEED)—to withdraw; the eleven states seceded from the Union and formed the Confederacy.

Yankee (YANG-kee)—nickname for a person in New England; people from Connecticut are sometimes called Connecticut Yankees.

To Learn More

Bagley, Katie. *Eli Whitney: American Inventor*. Let Freedom Ring. Mankato, Minn.: Bridgestone Books, 2003.

Bailer, Darice. *Connecticut, the Constitution State*. World Almanac Library of the States. Milwaukee: World Almanac Library, 2002.

Furstinger, Nancy. *Connecticut*. From Sea to Shining Sea. New York: Children's Press, 2002.

Gelman, Amy. *Connecticut*. Hello U.S.A. Minneapolis: Lerner Publications, 2002.

Internet Sites

Track down many sites about Connecticut.
Visit the FACT HOUND at *http://www.facthound.com*

IT IS EASY! IT IS FUN!
1) Go to *http://www.facthound.com*
2) Type in: 0736815759
3) Click on "FETCH IT" and FACT HOUND will find several links hand-picked by our editors.

Relax and let our pal FACT HOUND do the research for you!

Places to Write and Visit

Connecticut Office of Tourism
505 Hudson Street
Hartford, CT 06106-7106

Governor's Office
State Capitol
210 Capitol Avenue
Hartford, CT 06106

Mashantucket Pequot Museum and Research Center
110 Pequot Trail
P.O. Box 3180
Mashantucket, CT 06339-3180

Peabody Museum of Natural History
Yale University
P.O. Box 208118
170 Whitney Avenue
New Haven, CT 06520-8118

Wadsworth Atheneum Museum of Art
600 Main Street
Hartford, CT 06103

Connecticut is known for its beautiful New England scenery. Old stone bridges can be found throughout the state.